INSIDE COLLEGE
FOOTBALL

LSU TIGERS

BY ROBERT COOPER

SportsZone

An Imprint of Abdo Publishing
abdobooks.com

abdobooks.com

Published by Abdo Publishing, a division of ABDO, PO Box 398166, Minneapolis, Minnesota 55439.

Printed in the United States of America, North Mankato, Minnesota
042020
092020

Cover Photo: Aaron M. Sprecher/AP Images
Interior Photos: Patrick Dennis/AP Images, 5; Vasha Hunt/AP Images, 7; Gerald Herbert/AP Images, 9; LSU/Collegiate Images/Getty Images, 11; AP Images, 14, 17, 18, 21, 25, 27; Jacob Harris/AP Images, 23; Andy Lyons/Getty Images Sport/Getty Images, 29, 43; John Russell/AP Images, 31; Steven Savioa/AP Images, 32; Dave Martin/AP Images, 35; Charlie Riedel/AP Images, 37; Jonathan Bachman/Cal Sport Media/AP Images, 39; Sue Ogrocki/AP Images, 41

Editor: Patrick Donnelly
Series Designer: Nikki Nordby

Library of Congress Control Number: 2019954382

Publisher's Cataloging-in-Publication Data

Names: Cooper, Robert, author.
Title: LSU Tigers / by Robert Cooper
Description: Minneapolis, Minnesota : Abdo Publishing, 2021 | Series: Inside college football | Includes online resources and index.
Identifiers: ISBN 9781532192432 (lib. bdg.) | ISBN 9781644944677 (pbk.) | ISBN 9781098210335 (ebook)
Subjects: LCSH: LSU Tigers (Football team)--Juvenile literature. | Universities and colleges--Athletics--Juvenile literature. | American football--Juvenile literature. | College sports--United States--History--Juvenile literature.
Classification: DDC 796.33263--dc23

TABLE OF CONTENTS

CHAPTER 1

BURROW LEADS THE WAY

Joe Burrow had a decision to make. As a talented high school quarterback in Ohio, he had hoped to play college football at Nebraska. But the Cornhuskers ignored him. Instead he found a roster spot with nearby Ohio State, one of the best programs in the country. After three years, however, Burrow was still buried on the depth chart. So in May 2018, he announced he was transferring to Louisiana State University (LSU).

The Tigers had been one of college football's elite teams over the previous two decades. But since losing the national title game in January 2012, LSU seemed to have lost some of its swagger. The Tigers were still good, to be sure. But they were never quite *national championship* good. Burrow helped change that.

After going 10–3 with Burrow as the starter in 2018, the Tigers switched to a new spread offense in 2019. The high-flying scheme

Joe Burrow helped the Tigers maximize their offensive output in 2019.

LSU
9
LSU

was a perfect fit for Burrow, who could throw accurate passes on the run to LSU's elite receivers, a group that included Justin Jefferson, Ja'Marr Chase, and Terrace Marshall.

Ranked sixth in the national preseason poll, LSU opened the season with eight straight victories. They included an early win at No. 9 Texas and home defeats of No. 7 Florida and ninth-ranked Auburn. That set up the biggest showdown of the year, with LSU going on the road to face top-ranked Alabama.

The Crimson Tide had won eight straight games against LSU, including a 29–0 blowout at home in 2018. This one proved different. With nearly 102,000 fans in attendance, Burrow picked apart the Tide defense. He threw for 393 yards and three touchdowns. He also rushed for 64 yards. Though Alabama's offense put up a fight, the Tigers held on to win 46–41. No one was questioning LSU now.

The Tigers were hardly tested the rest of the way. They put up 58, 56, and 50 points in their last three regular-season games, winning each by more than 20 points. Then they clawed No. 4 Georgia 37–10 in the Southeastern Conference (SEC) title game.

When it was time to award the Heisman Trophy to college football's best player in December, Burrow was the overwhelming favorite. And he indeed won it—in historic fashion. A record 90.7 percent of voters picked Burrow to win. Meanwhile, Chase and cornerback Derek Stingley Jr. joined Burrow as first-team All-Americans.

An LSU fan holds a championship belt as he celebrates the Tigers' victory at Alabama.

The Tigers still had business to take care of, though. Since the 2014 season, the nation's top four teams have been selected to compete in the College Football Playoff (CFP). Behind Burrow, the top-ranked Tigers made the CFP field for the first time. And in the semifinal, they destroyed the fourth-ranked Oklahoma Sooners in the Peach Bowl. Burrow passed for a career-high 493 yards and

HEISMAN FOR GOOD

On December 14, 2019, Joe Burrow became the second LSU player to win the Heisman Trophy. In his speech, he talked about challenges facing his hometown of Athens, Ohio, where many people struggle with poverty and hunger. Soon a fundraiser began for a local food shelf. It raised more than $50,000 in just one day. Within a week, nearly $500,000 had been raised to help families in need.

seven touchdowns—including four to Jefferson in the first half—as the Tigers cruised to a 63–28 win.

That brought LSU to the date circled on its calendar. The CFP National Championship Game would be held just down the road from campus in New Orleans. In the other semifinal, No. 3 Clemson had toppled Ohio State, Burrow's former team. But Clemson would be no pushover. The *other* Tigers had reached three of the past four national title games, winning twice. They came to New Orleans riding a 29-game winning streak.

Clemson's experience showed early. It jumped out to a 17–7 lead in the second quarter. After that, the team's stout defense just needed to hold on. But with Burrow heating up, that was easier said than done. The LSU quarterback ran for a short touchdown. Then he hit Chase and tight end Thaddeus Moss for two more touchdowns before halftime. Although Clemson answered to come within three points early in the third quarter, that was as close as it would get. Burrow guided his offense like it was a video game, with the Tigers breaking out big plays just about every drive. The quarterback went on to throw touchdown passes to Moss and Marshall as LSU won easily, 42–25.

✕ LSU rode Burrow's right arm to its fourth national championship.

With the LSU faithful out in force to cheer them on, the Tigers celebrated the school's fourth national title and one of the greatest college football seasons ever—both for LSU and for Burrow. The Tigers became just the second team in football's top division since 1978 to finish a season 15–0. Their seven wins over top-10 teams set a record, as did their 726 points scored on the season. Burrow, meanwhile, finished the season with 5,671 passing yards, tied for the third-most ever, and a record 60 touchdown passes.

Wide receiver Marshall summed it up simply: "I think we're the greatest of all time. It's unbelievable."

CHAPTER 2

TO THE SUGAR BOWL AND BEYOND

The first college football game was played between Rutgers and Princeton in New Jersey in 1869. A little more than 20 years later, LSU played its first game. In 1893 LSU faced Tulane, which is in New Orleans, approximately 80 miles (129 km) from LSU's campus in Baton Rouge. Today LSU is a powerhouse, while Tulane plays in a smaller conference. But their fortunes were reversed in that first game, as Tulane won 34–0. That was LSU's only game of the season.

Many sports teams use "Tigers" as a nickname. Some are simply named after the ferocious felines. However, the LSU Tigers actually have a basis in history. During the American Civil War, military units in Louisiana were nicknamed "Tigers." In fact, the Washington Artillery of New Orleans even used a tiger head as

Doc Fenton became a star quarterback for LSU after moving from end in 1908.

its symbol. So it made sense for LSU's sports teams to be named the Tigers.

In 1908 LSU went undefeated in 10 games. The star of that team was Doc Fenton. Tigers coach Edgar Wingard recruited Fenton from Scranton, Pennsylvania. Fenton had played as an end. In 1908 the team switched him to quarterback. Fenton was not happy about making the change. However, Wingard helped encourage him by giving him $70 to buy some clothes in downtown Baton Rouge. That might have been against college rules—even back then.

The undefeated Tigers were known for the skillful way they tossed the ball around on laterals. They sometimes used two or

MAKING HISTORY IN CUBA

On Christmas Day in 1907, LSU became the first college football team to play a game in another country. The Tigers took on the University of Havana in Havana, Cuba. The game became known as the Bacardi Bowl.

Cuba isn't much known for football today. At the time, however, Havana's football team had beaten teams from the US military. The LSU players were undersized compared with their Cuban opponents. But the Tigers' ball skills and elusive running ability proved superior. LSU shut out Havana 56–0. This delighted the large number of US military members in attendance at the game.

The star of the day was LSU quarterback Doc Fenton. The Cubans called Fenton *El Rubio Vaselino* for his red hair and slippery moves on the field.

three laterals on a single play. As for Fenton, he was handy at tossing the ball, and he was a hard-to-catch runner. One of LSU's presidents, General Troy Middleton, said Fenton compared well with Jim Thorpe. Many consider Thorpe to be the greatest football player and athlete in the first half of the 20th century.

After the 10–0 season, the next big event in LSU football history came in 1924, when the school opened Tiger Stadium. It remains the Tigers' home today. LSU's first game at Tiger Stadium was against Tulane in the 1924 season finale. The stadium originally seated 12,000 fans. However, several additions were completed over the years. By 2019 its capacity was 102,321. That made it the fifth-biggest college football stadium in the country.

LSU played in the Southern Intercollegiate Athletic Association, which changed its name to the Southern Conference in the early 1920s. It had as many as 23 schools at its peak. Before the 1933 football season, 13 schools—including LSU—broke away to form the SEC. Today, some original members have left and other teams have joined. However, the SEC has always contained LSU's biggest football rivals: Alabama, Auburn, Florida, Georgia, and Mississippi.

On January 1, 1935, New Orleans began to host an annual postseason football game called the Sugar Bowl. It remains one of the most prestigious bowl games. LSU was not invited to the first Sugar Bowl, but the Tigers went to the next three. And even though LSU lost each time, it was the beginning of a successful run under coach Bernie Moore. All-America end Gus Tinsley led Moore's first

All-American Gus Tinsley, shown in 1935, starred for LSU as both a pass rusher and a pass catcher.

Sugar Bowl teams. In those days, players were used on both offense and defense. Tinsley was a valuable pass catcher and pass rusher.

LSU had played Texas Christian University (TCU) in its first Sugar Bowl game after the 1935 season. Tinsley chased after TCU's

All-America quarterback, Sammy Baugh. However, with muddy conditions neither team had much success on offense. The Tigers' only points came when Tinsley forced Baugh into a safety while Baugh was trying to pass. TCU ended up winning 3–2.

The Tigers lost more than the game that day. They had gone 9–1 during the regular season. Had they won the Sugar Bowl, they might have been named national champions.

LSU had another opportunity in the 1936 season. The Tigers finished the regular season ranked second in the country. But they again fell in the Sugar Bowl. This time Santa Clara won 21–14. LSU lost to Santa Clara in the Sugar Bowl the next season, too.

After the Sugar Bowl following the 1937 season, Moore kept the Tigers winning. They had only two losing records during his 13 seasons. They also won a bowl game for the first time, defeating Texas A&M 19–14 in the Orange Bowl after the 1943 season.

Moore took the Tigers to the Cotton Bowl after they went 9–1 in 1946. That Cotton Bowl against Arkansas was another postseason game the Tigers had to play in miserable conditions. This time it was ice, sleet, and snow. Neither offense could gain much traction, and the game ended in a 0–0 tie. LSU's quarterback that day was junior Y. A. Tittle. He would go on to a long career in the National Football League (NFL) and be inducted into the Pro Football Hall of Fame.

Moore coached one more season. Then his former player, Tinsley, replaced him as head coach in 1948. Fans hoped he would be as good a coach as he was as a player.

CHAPTER 3

MARCHING TO A TITLE

Former LSU star Gus Tinsley took over as the Tigers' head coach in 1948. In 1949 Tinsley directed LSU back to the Sugar Bowl after posting an 8–2 regular-season record. However, Oklahoma pounded the Tigers 35–0 in New Orleans on January 2, 1950, and that was the last bowl game for LSU under Tinsley. The Tigers had losing records in three of the next five seasons.

Tinsley's last season was 1954. All-America senior tackle Sid Fournet was that team's star on both offense and defense. Fournet was on the field for 83 percent of the Tigers' plays that season.

But LSU needed a change. In 1955 Paul Dietzel took over for Tinsley. At age 31, Dietzel became the youngest head coach in the country. But he arrived in Baton Rouge with plenty of experience. Dietzel had served as an assistant coach at Army. He had prepared for his first head coaching job by working under and alongside

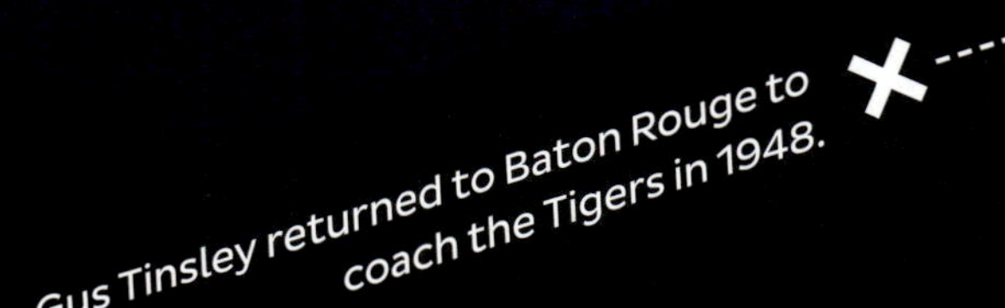

Gus Tinsley returned to Baton Rouge to coach the Tigers in 1948.

Tigers coach Paul Dietzel, *right*, speaks to his players in 1958. He installed a unique rotation system at LSU.

some of the greatest coaches of all time. His mentors included Red Blaik, Bear Bryant, Vince Lombardi, and Sid Gillman.

Dietzel installed a unique system of rotating players into and out of the game. The White Team was the starting offense and defense. The Go Team was the second-string offense. And the Chinese Bandits formed the second-string defense.

In his first three seasons, Dietzel had records of 3–5–2, 3–7, and 5–5. The best player for LSU during that time was fullback Jim Taylor. He became better known for his NFL days with Lombardi's Green Bay Packers. But Taylor first showed off his bruising running style for the Tigers. He often tried to run directly into a would-be tackler rather than around him.

CHINESE BANDITS

How did coach Paul Dietzel come up with the name "Chinese Bandits" for his second-team defense? It originated from a popular comic strip called *Terry and the Pirates*. A character in the comic said Chinese bandits were "the most vicious people on Earth." That was the kind of toughness Dietzel wanted from his players.

"I tried to initiate the contact," Taylor said. "That might be a little bit different than the normal running back. . . . If you drop down and initiate the contact with that cornerback or linebacker, I might pick up another 18 inches—which may make the difference in measuring for a first down."

Taylor led the SEC in rushing yards once and in scoring twice, 1956 and 1957. The team only kept improving in 1958. Junior running back Billy Cannon led the Tigers. He possessed a combination of speed and strength that made him unique in college football.

"Billy's by far the best athlete I've ever coached," Dietzel said. "He's stronger, faster, tougher. He can do more things well. And he improves from week to week. Give him a step and he's gone. But if there's no room, he'll run over you. When he does, it hurts."

Cannon also played defense, did some of the kicking, and threw the occasional pass. The Chinese Bandits defensive unit played a big role in the 1958 team, too. Those players were not as talented as the first-team players. But they made up for it with their high spirit. In fact, players who were promoted to the White Team often wanted to stay as members of the Bandits.

The Bandits, with their swarming, gang-tackling style, helped LSU record four shutouts during that 1958 season. None was more important than the 14–0 victory over Mississippi in the seventh game of the season. LSU had moved into the number-one spot in the national rankings the week before. The showdown drew the first sellout crowd to fill the 67,500 seats in Tiger Stadium. The key series came in the second quarter. Mississippi had four tries to score from LSU's 2-yard line, but the offense was unable to cross the goal line.

The Tigers went on to finish the regular season undefeated at 10–0. All that was left for LSU was a Sugar Bowl showdown against Clemson. However, the final polls back then actually came before bowl games. So the most respected polls all named LSU as the national champions before the Sugar Bowl. But LSU did not let up in that bowl game. Cannon threw a touchdown pass for the game's only score. The Tigers defeated Clemson 7–0 to cap off their first national championship season.

Cannon held a special place in the school's football history after that 1958 season. As a senior in 1959, he added to his legacy.

LSU running back Billy Cannon runs through Mississippi defenders on an 89-yard punt return in 1959.

On Halloween night, Cannon made what many consider the most famous play in LSU football history. LSU trailed rival Mississippi 3–0 in the fourth quarter. Then Cannon ran back a punt 89 yards for a touchdown. He showed off the qualities that made him such

a terrific player. Cannon's strength allowed him to break several attempted tackles. Then his speed carried him to the end zone. His touchdown provided the margin of victory in a 7–3 win.

"That was the greatest run I ever saw in football," Dietzel later recalled.

The Tigers finished the 1959 season with another appearance in the Sugar Bowl. This time, LSU lost in a rematch with Mississippi. With a 9–2 record, the Tigers finished the season ranked third. Although they did not win another national championship, Cannon

FIGHTING OVER CANNON

Professional football was just beginning to truly take off in 1959, when Heisman Trophy winner Billy Cannon played his final year at LSU. The American Football League (AFL) was created in 1960 to challenge the established NFL.

One of the ways the AFL and NFL fought each other was over players. Both leagues wanted Cannon. He ended up signing contracts with the Los Angeles Rams of the NFL and the Houston Oilers of the AFL.

The matter of the two contracts ended up in court, and Cannon ended up going to the Oilers. It was the AFL's first big victory in its fight for a spot on the pro football landscape. Cannon also played for the Oakland Raiders and the Kansas City Chiefs during his 11 years in professional football. After starting out as a running back in college, Cannon switched to tight end with the Raiders.

Running back Billy Cannon became the first LSU player to win the Heisman Trophy in 1959.

won that year's Heisman Trophy as the best player in college football. He became the first LSU player to win that honor.

Dietzel coached two more seasons at LSU. In his final year, he led the 1961 Tigers to a 10–1 record, an Orange Bowl berth, and a final ranking of number four. And the winning tradition would only grow with the next coach.

CHAPTER 4

CONSISTENTLY GOOD

Charlie McClendon, who had been an assistant to Paul Dietzel, took over as head coach in 1962. Over the next 18 years, he became LSU's winningest coach, posting a 137–59–7 record.

Halfback Jerry Stovall led the way for McClendon in 1962. A versatile player, he also returned kicks and punts and even played some defensive back en route to being the runner-up for the Heisman Trophy. In the Cotton Bowl, Stovall and the Tigers upset previously unbeaten Texas to finish the season 9–1–1.

LSU became a regular participant in bowl games in the coming years. One of the most memorable was the Cotton Bowl after the 1965 season. Arkansas came into the game undefeated. McClendon decided to motivate his Tigers by having the players on the practice team wear red like Arkansas. But he took it a step further.

Charlie McClendon, LSU's all-time winningest coach, was inducted into the College Football Hall of Fame in 1986.

THE RUSTON RIFLE

Bert Jones did not become a starting quarterback at LSU until the very end of his junior season. By his senior year in 1972, he was ready to make a big impact. Jones, a native of Ruston, Louisiana, finished fourth in voting for the Heisman Trophy and was named to several All-America teams. Jones's biggest play at LSU came against rival Mississippi. His touchdown pass on the last play of the game gave the Tigers a 17–16 victory.

"Arkansas had won 22 straight games, and for two weeks in our preparation we had red jerseys for our scout squad and all the numbers on them were 23," McClendon said. "We just said, 'Fellas, you are going to be victim number 23 if they beat us.' After a while, that irritated the guys something awful."

LSU did not become number 23. The Tigers defeated Arkansas 14–7.

Five years later, in 1970, McClendon coached the Tigers to a 9–3 record and a spot in the Orange Bowl. The Tigers finished the season ranked seventh in the nation. McClendon, for his part, was named co-National Coach of the Year.

The United States had been segregated for most of its history. Many southern universities' football teams remained all-white through the 1960s and into the early 1970s. That changed at LSU in 1973. Lora Hinton became the Tigers' first black player when McClendon offered him a football scholarship. Hinton said some areas around the LSU campus still did not want to admit black people, but his teammates would not allow him to be excluded. "When the team went there, they made sure that I was there, and

LSU quarterback Bert Jones tries to get past a Rice defender during a 1972 game in Houston, Texas.

if anybody had any problem with that, they had to deal with those guys. That's just the way it was," Hinton said.

Although McClendon's teams continued to win, they struggled to get past rival Alabama. McClendon's teams went just 2–14 against Bear Bryant's Crimson Tide. "That was a sore spot with a lot of people," McClendon said. "But there weren't many people beating [Alabama] in those days." After the 1979 season, he resigned.

ALEXANDER THE GREAT

Charles Alexander followed Billy Cannon as the next elite LSU running back. He rushed for more than 1,000 yards in his junior and senior seasons and set 27 LSU records by the end of his career in 1978. In a 1977 game against Oregon, Alexander ran for 237 yards and scored four touchdowns. He went on to the NFL and played in a Super Bowl with the Cincinnati Bengals. "Make sure to capitalize the 'G' on 'Great,' because that's exactly what he was for us," LSU coach Charlie McClendon said.

Bo Rein was hired away from North Carolina State to replace McClendon. But Rein never coached a game at LSU. He died in an airplane crash while on a recruiting trip in January 1980.

Former LSU star Jerry Stovall then became head coach. His 1982 team achieved a number 11 ranking and went to the Orange Bowl. But after posting just two winning seasons in four years, not even Stovall's popularity in Louisiana could save his job.

Bill Arnsparger replaced Stovall. The veteran coach took the Tigers to the Sugar Bowl after the 1984 and 1986 seasons. They also won the SEC championship in 1986. However, he retired after just three seasons and became the athletic director at Florida.

Mike Archer, one of Arnsparger's top assistants, replaced him, and the future looked bright. The 1987 team went 10–1–1, and its number five final ranking was LSU's highest since 1961. The Tigers shared the SEC championship the next season and went to another bowl game. But in 1989 LSU began a string of six consecutive losing seasons.

Running back Kevin Faulk (3) and guard Alan Faneca (66) starred at LSU in the mid-1990s.

In 1995 Gerry DiNardo got LSU back on a winning track. The Tigers played in bowl games three straight seasons and returned to the national rankings. DiNardo's first teams featured explosive running back Kevin Faulk and a solid blocker in guard Alan Faneca. Both went on to make big impacts in the NFL. However, DiNardo closed out the 1990s with two losing seasons. He was gone after five years in Baton Rouge. But as the 2000s began, LSU was about to start its greatest decade of football yet.

CHAPTER 5

AMONG THE ELITE

The Tigers have had periods of great success in their history. But they were never as consistently elite as they were in the period that began in 2000. Over the next 20 seasons, the Tigers went on to win three national titles and play in 20 bowl games.

The rise began after the 1999 season, when LSU hired Nick Saban as head coach. He had an impressive career before that, including five years leading Michigan State's program.

Right away Saban guided his team to an 8–4 record and a win in the Peach Bowl. LSU ended the year ranked twenty-second. One year later, senior quarterback Rohan Davey and junior wide receiver Josh Reed helped the Tigers finish 10–3 after beating Illinois in the Sugar Bowl. That left them seventh in the final rankings, the team's best finish since 1987.

LSU running back Domanick Davis leaps over a Tennessee player during a kick return in a 2001 game.

LSU
31

LSU wide receiver Josh Reed makes a catch in the 2002 Sugar Bowl against Illinois.

Though LSU ended the next year 8–5 and out of the top 25 at season's end, they took a huge step in 2003. Few were expecting a breakout season that year. Junior quarterback Matt Mauck was coming off an injury suffered in the previous season. Meanwhile, game-changing linebacker Bradie James had left for the NFL and the team's top two running backs also had departed.

LSU entered the season ranked 14th in the nation and rolled through its first three games. That bumped the Tigers' ranking up to No. 11 going into their first big test, against seventh-ranked Georgia. LSU had not beaten Georgia in 13 years. In a tight game, LSU did not

take the lead for good until Mauck hit Skyler Green for a touchdown with less than 1:30 left on the clock. The Tigers held on for the 17–10 victory.

An easy win over Mississippi State moved LSU up to No. 6. Although Florida came to Baton Rouge and upset the Tigers 19–7, Saban's team pressed on. The Tigers toppled their next six opponents to finish 11–1. Then they cruised past No. 5 Georgia 34–13 in an SEC title game rematch. LSU jumped to No. 2 in the nation and earned a berth in the Bowl Championship Series (BCS) National Championship Game against Oklahoma.

The Sooners featured Heisman Trophy–winning quarterback Jason White. But the Tigers were not intimidated. That year's title game was a familiar setting for LSU—the Sugar Bowl. And the Tigers played like they were at home.

White completed only 13 of his 37 passes. He threw two interceptions and was sacked five times. Junior defensive end

DBU

During the 2000s, LSU established a reputation for developing great defensive backs. This led to the school taking on the nickname Defensive Back University, or DBU. From 2005 through 2019, NFL teams selected more than 20 former LSU defensive backs in the draft. Few were better than Patrick Peterson. Drafted by Arizona No. 5 overall in 2011, Peterson became an All-Pro cornerback. Corey Webster (2005, 43rd pick), Tyrann Mathieu (2013, 69th pick), Eric Reid (2013, 18th pick), LaRon Landry (2007, sixth pick), and Morris Claiborne (2012, sixth pick) are among the other former LSU defensive backs to thrive in the NFL.

Marcus Spears returned one of those interceptions for a touchdown. That was enough to secure LSU's 21–14 win.

The win meant LSU was the BCS national champion. But the Associated Press poll determined that the University of Southern California (USC) was the sport's best team. Because of that, LSU's second national title was officially shared with the Trojans.

Although the Tigers came into the 2004 season ranked fourth in the country, they ended up finishing 9–3 and sixteenth in the nation. Even worse, though, was that they lost their coach. Saban left to become coach of the NFL's Miami Dolphins.

Saban had lifted LSU back among the elite. Les Miles took over with the goal of keeping them there. Miles was coming off a successful head coaching stint at Oklahoma State. And he picked up right where Saban left off at LSU.

Sophomore quarterback JaMarcus Russell led LSU to an 11–2 record in 2005. The Tigers finished the season ranked sixth overall. That was followed by another 11–2 record in 2006, along with a Sugar Bowl spot and a number three ranking. Fans were eager for the team to take that next step, though.

The 2007 season began on a high note. The Tigers opened the season ranked second in the country. They started things off with a 45–0 shutout over Mississippi State. And they continued to win. By their sixth game, the Tigers were ranked number one in the nation. And they held on to that ranking after beating ninth-ranked Florida 28–24.

LSU running back Justin Vincent runs for a touchdown during the Tigers' win over Oklahoma in the 2004 BCS title game.

The Tigers stumbled in their next game, losing 43–37 in triple overtime at Kentucky. But they won their next two games, both over ranked opponents, and by their eleventh game were back to No. 1 in the country. However, LSU's regular-season finale against Arkansas again went to three overtimes. And once again the Tigers fell, this time 50–48. With those two triple-overtime losses, their hopes for a national title appeared to be over.

LSU went into the SEC title game ranked No. 5 in the nation. A lot would have to happen for the Tigers to jump back up into the

PICKING TALENT

Seven LSU players were selected in the 2008 National Football League (NFL) Draft. One of them, defensive tackle Glenn Dorsey, went fifth overall to the Kansas City Chiefs. Three more players went in the third round. They were cornerback Chevis Jackson, fullback Jacob Hester, and wide receiver Early Doucet. Safety Craig Steltz was picked in the fourth round, and quarterback Matt Flynn and tight end Keith Zinger both went in the seventh round.

top two. Then it all started happening. Top-ranked Missouri lost. No. 2 West Virginia fell, too. Meanwhile, LSU held off Tennessee 21–14. It was the fewest points LSU had scored all year. But LSU jumped up to second in the BCS rankings. That set up a meeting with Ohio State in the BCS National Championship Game.

"By the grace of God we got here," Miles said. "Once we got here, we were going to do our best."

Once again the game was back in New Orleans. Ohio State jumped out to a 10–0 lead. It was all LSU from there. The Tigers scored 31 consecutive points. Senior quarterback Matt Flynn threw four touchdown passes in the game. Senior defensive back Chevis Jackson also played a major role. He batted away a sure touchdown pass when the game was still tied in the first half. In the end, the Tigers won 38–24 to claim their third national title. They became the first team with two losses to win a BCS national title.

"We knew we had the opportunity to come out here and make history," senior defensive end Kirston Pittman said. "We're the first

× LSU cornerback Chevis Jackson runs after intercepting an Ohio State pass during the 2008 BCS title game.

team to win two BCS championships. We're the winningest class in LSU history."

Though the Tigers did not make the top 25 in the final 2008 rankings, it was a temporary setback. In 2009 and 2010, they won a combined 20 games and were rated among the nation's best teams.

Then LSU returned to the top of the rankings in 2011. Opening the season at No. 4 in the polls, the Tigers started their climb with a 40–27 win over third-ranked Oregon. The Ducks had been the national runners-up in 2010. LSU was ranked No. 1 by its fifth

LEONARD FOURNETTE

As a freshman in 2014, Leonard Fournette rushed for 1,034 yards. One year later he surpassed that total in just five games. The 6-foot-1, 230-pound Fournette ended with 1,953 rushing yards that year, breaking Charles Alexander's 38-year-old school record. Fournette's total might have been higher, but LSU's first game of the season was canceled due to weather. Nonetheless, his 158.3 rushing yards per game during the regular season led the nation. The biggest surprise was when he wasn't named a Heisman Trophy finalist. Fournette left LSU after the 2016 season, and the Jacksonville Jaguars picked him fourth in the 2017 NFL Draft.

game, and it held on to that ranking as it went undefeated through the regular season.

The biggest game on the schedule was in November at Alabama. The Crimson Tide came in ranked No 2. Saban had taken over as Alabama's coach. The game turned into a classic defensive struggle. In front of more than 100,000 fans, the teams went to overtime tied 6–6 before LSU finally won on a field goal.

LSU and Alabama were both in the SEC West. So only LSU went to the SEC Championship Game. But after LSU took care of business against Georgia in the SEC title game, it met a familiar foe in the BCS National Championship Game: Alabama.

The national title game was back in New Orleans. And once again, defense dominated. Unfortunately for LSU, Alabama's defense came out on top. The Crimson Tide won 21–0, and the Tigers finished the season ranked number two.

LSU cornerback Tyrann Mathieu finished fifth in the 2011 Heisman Trophy voting.

Saban had brought the Tigers back among the nation's elite. Then Miles built upon Saban's success. LSU was established as one of the nation's premier programs. And expectations continued to soar.

The Tigers went into the 2013 season ranked third in the nation. However, losses to Florida and Alabama, and then to Clemson in the Chick-fil-A Bowl, left the Tigers 10–3 and fourteenth in the nation.

After that, LSU remained good but was never quite among the nation's best under Miles. The 2013 team featured star wide receiver Odell Beckham Jr. He had 59 catches for 1,152 yards and hauled in

ED ORGERON

Ed Orgeron took over as LSU's head coach during the 2016 season when Les Miles was fired. The school hired him full time after that season. A Louisiana native, Orgeron grew up cheering for the Tigers and briefly played for the team. Orgeron's first foray into head coaching was a forgettable three-year stint at Ole Miss. He also coached at USC for one season. He said those experiences prepared him for his dream job coaching the Tigers. "I wanted to come back to be the best football coach I could possibly be when I took this job, and I feel like that happened," he said. "I'm prepared to do it."

eight touchdown passes. The Tigers won 10 games and reached as high as sixth in the national rankings. However, they again ended the season ranked fourteenth.

Beckham left for the NFL after that. Freshman running back Leonard Fournette stepped up in 2014. He rushed for 1,034 yards and 10 touchdowns, but the Tigers finished just 8–5. One year later, Fournette ran for 1,953 yards and 22 touchdowns. But the Tigers won only one more game.

Though Miles had led the Tigers to a national title, fans were becoming frustrated. They watched as other teams adopted explosive offenses while Miles stuck to his old-fashioned, grind-it-out approach. LSU finished 9–3 in 2015, well outside the national championship picture. When the Tigers started the next season 2–2, the school decided to put an end to the Miles era.

Ed Orgeron took over mid-season and led the Tigers to an 8–4 record, followed by 9–4 in 2017. Then, in 2018, the team stepped back into the spotlight. The Tigers opened the season by upsetting

Ed Orgeron, LSU's fiery head coach, led the Tigers to the 2019 national title.

eighth-ranked Miami at the Dallas Cowboys' stadium. Eventually the team climbed as high as fourth in the rankings before being shut out 29–0 against top-ranked Alabama. Still, the Tigers finished out the season with a win over seventh-ranked Central Florida in the Fiesta Bowl to finish 10–3.

That set up an even bigger 2019, when quarterback Joe Burrow led LSU to an undefeated record and a fourth national title. That win cemented the Tigers' place among college football's elite. Fans hoped it was the start of another long era of success in Baton Rouge.

TIMELINE

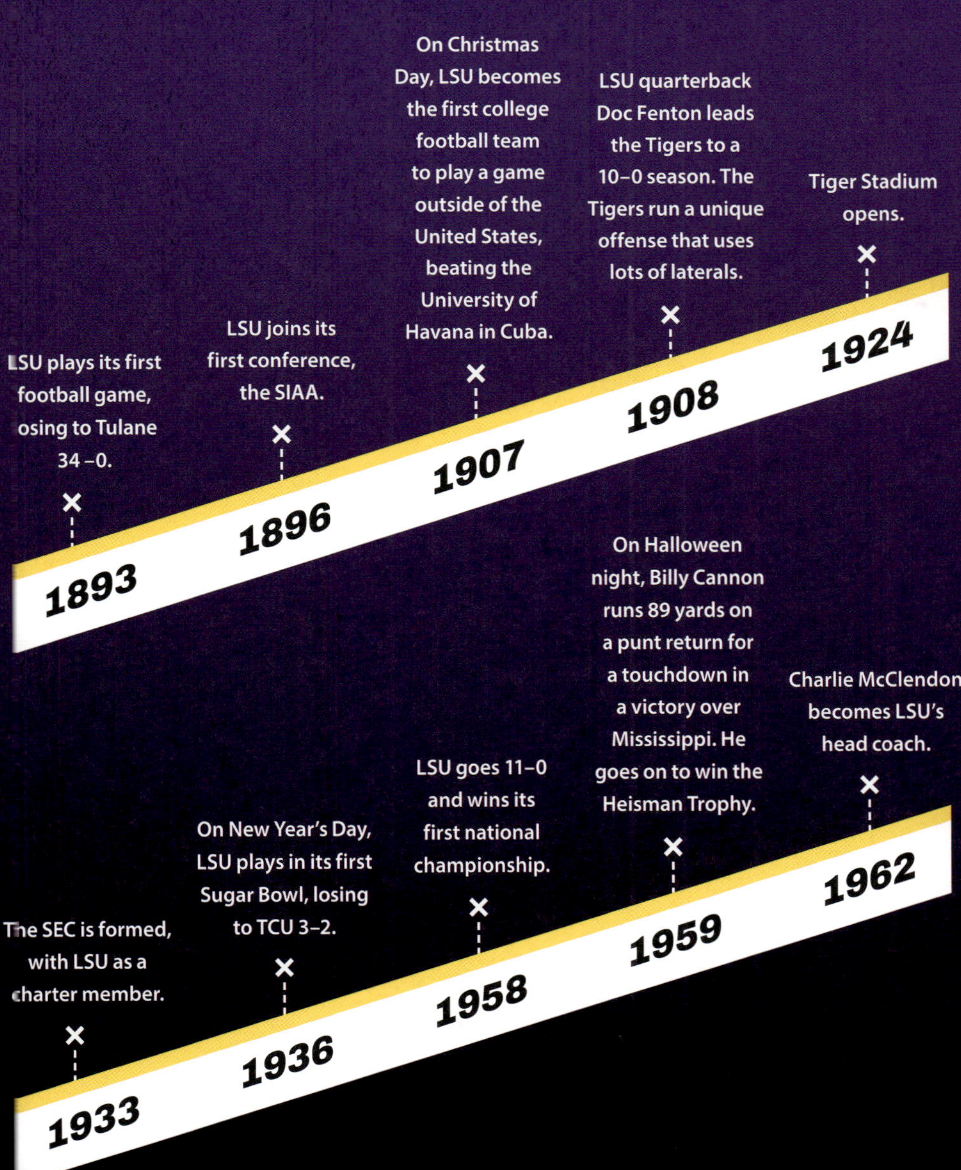

1893
LSU plays its first football game, losing to Tulane 34–0.

1896
LSU joins its first conference, the SIAA.

1907
On Christmas Day, LSU becomes the first college football team to play a game outside of the United States, beating the University of Havana in Cuba.

1908
LSU quarterback Doc Fenton leads the Tigers to a 10–0 season. The Tigers run a unique offense that uses lots of laterals.

1924
Tiger Stadium opens.

1933
The SEC is formed, with LSU as a charter member.

1936
On New Year's Day, LSU plays in its first Sugar Bowl, losing to TCU 3–2.

1958
LSU goes 11–0 and wins its first national championship.

1959
On Halloween night, Billy Cannon runs 89 yards on a punt return for a touchdown in a victory over Mississippi. He goes on to win the Heisman Trophy.

1962
Charlie McClendon becomes LSU's head coach.

1973 Lora Hinton becomes LSU's first black football player.

1989 A year after sharing the SEC title, LSU begins a streak of six straight losing seasons.

2000 Nick Saban takes over as LSU's head coach and turns the Tigers into a contender.

2004 LSU beats Oklahoma in the Sugar Bowl on January 4 to win the BCS national championship.

2005 Les Miles takes over as head coach.

2008 The 11–2 Tigers beat Ohio State in the BCS National Championship Game on January 7.

2012 LSU reaches the BCS National Championship Game but falls to SEC rival Alabama on January 9.

2016 After a 2–2 start, Miles is fired as head coach and replaced by Louisiana native Ed Orgeron.

2018 On November 24, LSU and Texas A&M play long into the night before A&M pulls out a 74–72 victory in seven overtimes.

2019 Quarterback Joe Burrow wins the Heisman Trophy and leads LSU to an undefeated season to win the school's fourth national championship.

QUICK STATS

PROGRAM INFO

Louisiana State University Tigers (1893–)

NATIONAL CHAMPIONSHIPS

1958, 2003*, 2007, 2019

OTHER ACHIEVEMENTS

CFP appearances (2014–): 2019
SEC championships (1933–): 11
Bowl record: 28–23–1

KEY COACHES

Paul Dietzel (1955–61)
46–24–3, 2–1 (bowl games)
Charlie McClendon (1962–79)
37–59–7, 7–6 (bowl games)
Les Miles (2005–16)
114–34, 8–4 (bowl games)
Ed Orgeron (2016–)
40–9, 4–1 (bowl games)

KEY PLAYERS

Charles Alexander (RB, 1975–78)
Odell Beckham Jr. (WR, 2011–13)
Joe Burrow (QB, 2018–19)**
Billy Cannon (HB/DB, 1957–59)**
Warren Capone (LB, 1971–73)
Tommy Casanova (RB/DB, 1969–71)
Glenn Dorsey (DT, 2004–07)
Kevin Faulk (RB, 1995–98)
Leonard Fournette (RB, 2014–16)
Bradie James (LB, 1999–2002)
Bert Jones (QB, 1970–72)
Tyrann Mathieu (DB, 2010–11)
Josh Reed (WR, 1999–2001)
Jerry Stovall (RB/DB, 1960–62)
Gus Tinsley (E, 1934–36)

HOME STADIUM

Tiger Stadium (1924–)

*Denotes shared title
**Heisman Trophy winner
All statistics through 2019 season

QUOTES AND ANECDOTES

"This team is full of grown men, guys who've been there before, guys who never quit. We just knew we had to keep going. We had a lot of time. We just had to keep moving along just like we've done all year."

—Matt Flynn, quarterback of the 2007 national champion team

During LSU's 10–0 season in 1908, the Tigers defeated Auburn 10–2. Auburn's only points came on a safety, when it blocked a punt by LSU's star, Doc Fenton, in the end zone. Fenton said after the block that he was trying to pick up the bouncing ball when an Auburn fan interfered. The fans were right next to the field in the end zone, separated from the players by only a rope. "A fan reached over the rope and cracked me on the head with a cane," Fenton said. "It knocked me cold."

"With the ball under his arm, Jimmy Taylor was the best running back I've ever coached. He was just so versatile."

—LSU coach Paul Dietzel

The first live Mike the Tiger mascot arrived on the LSU campus in 1936. He was purchased from a zoo in Little Rock, Arkansas. The tiger was named Mike in honor of LSU's athletic director, Mike Chambers. He was the man behind the effort to get the tiger. The first Mike lived to be 20. Others followed. The seventh Mike the Tiger took over in September 2016.

The Tigers lost the longest—and highest-scoring—game in their history on November 24, 2018. Host Texas A&M pulled out a 74–72 victory in seven overtimes. The game was tied 31–31 after regulation.

GLOSSARY

All-American
A player chosen as one of the best amateurs in the country in a particular sport.

athletic director
An administrator who oversees an institution's coaches, players, and teams.

conference
In sports, a group of teams that play each other each season.

draft
A system that allows teams to acquire new players coming into a league.

lateral
A pass thrown parallel to or away

rival
An opponent with whom a player or team has a fierce and ongoing competition.

sack
In football, tackling the quarterback behind the line of scrimmage when he is trying to pass.

scholarship
Financial assistance awarded to students to help them pay for school.

segregated
Separated or divided from each other, often enforced by law.

MORE INFORMATION

BOOKS

Graves, Will. *The Story of the Sugar Bowl*. Minneapolis, MN: Abdo Publishing, 2016.

Wilner, Barry. *The Story of the College Football National Championship Game*. Minneapolis, MN: Abdo Publishing, 2016.

York, Andy. *Ultimate College Football Road Trip*. Minneapolis, MN: Abdo Publishing, 2019.

ONLINE RESOURCES

To learn more about the LSU Tigers, please visit **abdobooklinks.com** or scan this QR code. These links are routinely monitored and updated to provide the most current information available.

PLACES TO VISIT

College Football Hall of Fame
cfbhall.com

This hall of fame and museum in Atlanta, Georgia, highlights the greatest players and moments in the history of college football. Among the former Tigers enshrined here are Charles Alexander, Billy Cannon, Charlie McClendon, and Jerry Stovall.

Tiger Stadium
lsusports.net/news/2018/10/19/177159.aspx

Opened as LSU's home stadium in 1924, Tiger Stadium seats more than 100,000 fans and is the fifth largest stadium in college football. Tiger Stadium is nicknamed "Death Valley."

INDEX

ABOUT THE AUTHOR

Robert Cooper is a retired law enforcement officer and lifelong football fan. He and his wife live in Seattle near their only son and two grandchildren.